pause & reflect

MEDITATIONS FOR HOPE

pause & reflect

MEDITATIONS FOR HOPE

ONE VOICE
PRESS

EVANSTON, ILLINOIS

One Voice Press
1233 Central St., Evanston, IL 60202

Printed in the United States of America on
acid-free paper ∞

ISBN: 978-1-61851-255-0
27 26 25 24   4 3 2 1

Cover design by Carlos Esparza
Book design by Patrick Falso

CONTENTS

INTRODUCTION

There is much in our modern world competing for our attention. Technology is changing at a pace so rapid that most of us cannot keep up, let alone take the time to process the ways in which it is affecting us. As we go about our daily lives we are seemingly assaulted with an endless series of distractions. The need to retreat from the stress and chaos that so often surrounds us, to center ourselves and reflect on our inner reality, has never been of more vital importance. It is with this in mind that One Voice Press is happy to present this, the sixth title in its *Pause & Reflect* series.

Pause & Reflect is a series that presents meditative passages from the writings of the Bahá'í Faith arranged around particular themes. While the Bahá'í Faith places a great deal of importance on meditation and the cultivation of spirituality, it is also a religion that calls for action and societal transformation. Meditation, from a Bahá'í perspective, is not exclusively a means for personal growth but also a tool that should equip us with insights and awareness that can be translated into action both in our lives and in the communities in which we live.

The theme of this volume is hope. There is little doubt that we are living in unsettling times, and it is easy to become overwhelmed by events unfolding in the world and to feel a sense of despair. However, according to the Bahá'í writings, this upheaval is serving a purpose essential to the advancement of civilization. We live in a momentous time in human history where humanity, in its collective growth, is experiencing the tumultuous phase of adolescence and is preparing to enter the stage of maturity. From a Bahá'í perspective, there are two types of forces at work during this transition—the forces of disintegration and the forces of integration. On the one hand, old institutions and ways of life are crumbling and proving inadequate and incompatible with the healthy advancement of humankind, and on the other hand, people throughout the world are uniting to work together and build new structures in their place.

The Bahá'í vision of the future is one of peace and prosperity in which the oneness of humanity is realized and justice is the prevailing principle. It is toward this goal that Bahá'ís all over the world, along with their friends and neighbors, are working. In every neighborhood and locality, Bahá'ís, along with likeminded collaborators, are engaged in a process of community building. Their actions are characterized by a spirit of service and animated by the twofold purpose of personal spiritual development and the transformation of society. To be engaged in this process is to consciously live a life of hope translated into action.

The sections of this book are arranged in three parts: hope through hardship and global unrest, hope for spiritual development, and hope for the future with an emphasis on peace, unity, and justice. Readers will find much to ponder and reflect upon within these pages. The passages collected here contain wisdom and truths that can imbue our lives with a hopeful and purposeful perspective capable of transforming our reality into one of hope— hope for our loved ones, for our communities, for the future of our planet, and for all of humanity.

Hope Through
Hardship &
Global Unrest

BAHÁ'U'LLÁH

1

If adversity befall thee not in My path, how canst thou walk in the ways of them that are content with My pleasure? If trials afflict thee not in thy longing to meet Me, how wilt thou attain the light in thy love for My beauty?

2

Whatever befalleth in the path of God is the beloved of the soul and the desire of the heart. Deadly poison in His path is pure honey, and every tribulation a draught of crystal water. . . . Verily God hath made adversity as a morning dew upon His green pasture, and a wick for His lamp which lighteth earth and heaven.

3

The world's equilibrium hath been upset through the vibrating influence of this most great, this new World Order. Mankind's ordered life hath been revolutionized through the agency of this unique, this wondrous System—the like of which mortal eyes have never witnessed.

4

In all matters moderation is desirable. If a thing is carried to excess, it will prove a source of evil. Consider the civilization of the West, how it hath agitated and alarmed the peoples of the world. An infernal engine hath been devised, and hath proved so cruel a weapon of destruction that its like none hath ever witnessed or heard. The purging of such deeply-rooted and overwhelming corruptions cannot be effected unless the peoples of the world unite in pursuit of one common aim and embrace one universal faith.

‘ABDU’L-BAHÁ

5

Never lose thy trust in God. Be thou ever hopeful, for the bounties of God never cease to flow upon man. If viewed from one perspective they seem to decrease, but from another they are full and complete. Man is under all conditions immersed in a sea of God's blessings. Therefore, be thou not hopeless under any circumstances, but rather be firm in thy hope.

6

When calamity striketh, be ye patient and composed. However afflictive your sufferings may be, stay ye undisturbed, and with perfect confidence in the abounding grace of God, brave ye the tempest of tribulations and fiery ordeals.

7

Even as Jesus Christ forfeited His life, may you, likewise, offer yourselves in the threshold of sacrifice for the betterment of the world; and just as Bahá'u'lláh suffered severe ordeals and calamities nearly fifty years for you, may you be willing to undergo difficulties and withstand catastrophes for humanity in general. May you bear these trials and tests most willingly and joyously, for every night is followed by a day, and every day has a night.

8

O Divine Providence! Perplexing difficulties have arisen and formidable obstacles have appeared. O Lord! Remove these difficulties and show forth the evidences of Thy might and power. Ease these hardships and smooth our way along this arduous path. O Divine Providence! The obstacles are unyielding, and our toil and hardship are conjoined with a myriad adversities. There is no helper save Thee, and no succourer except Thyself. We set all our hopes on Thee, and commit all our affairs unto Thy care. Thou art the Guide and the Remover of every difficulty, and Thou art the Wise, the Seeing, and the Hearing.

9

Rely upon God. Trust in Him. Praise Him, and call Him continually to mind. He verily turneth trouble into ease, and sorrow into solace, and toil into utter peace. He verily hath dominion over all things.

10

ODivine Providence! Grant me the strength to bear this heavy burden, and enable me to safeguard this supreme bestowal, for so strong is the force of tests and so grievous the onslaught of trials that every mountain is scattered in dust, and the highest peak reduced to nothing. Thou knowest full well that in my heart I seek naught but Thy remembrance, and in my soul I desire nothing save Thy love. Raise me up to serve Thy loved ones, and let me abide forever in servitude at Thy Threshold. Thou art the Loving. Thou art the Lord of manifold bounties.

11

Whosoever entereth the Kingdom of God is under the protection of Bahá'u'lláh. The changes and chances of the material world, whether good or bad, are like the waves of the sea, which pass away and are no more. They are not worthy of attention. . . . The denizens of the Kingdom derive their joy from the bounties of God and set their hopes on His infinite grace. They exult in the outpourings of divine bounty and are gladdened by the favours of the Lord of Hosts. In the fire of tribulations they remain fresh and verdant, and in the tempest of trials and afflictions tranquil and at peace, for they rest their backs against a mighty mountain and take refuge in a ship wrought of steel.

12

Othou who art turning thy face towards God! Close thine eyes to all things else, and open them to the realm of the All-Glorious. Ask whatsoever thou wishest of Him alone; seek whatsoever thou seekest from Him alone. With a look He granteth a hundred thousand hopes, with a glance He healeth a hundred thousand incurable ills, with a nod He layeth balm on every wound, with a glimpse He freeth the hearts from the shackles of grief. He doeth as He doeth, and what recourse have we? He carrieth out His Will, He ordaineth what He pleaseth. Then better for thee to bow down thy head in submission, and put thy trust in the All-Merciful Lord.

13

The mind and spirit of man advance when he is tried by suffering. The more the ground is ploughed the better the seed will grow, the better the harvest will be. Just as the plough furrows the earth deeply, purifying it of weeds and thistles, so suffering and tribulation free man from the petty affairs of this worldly life until he arrives at a state of complete detachment. His attitude in this world will be that of divine happiness. Man is, so to speak, unripe: the heat of the fire of suffering will mature him. Look back to the times past and you will find that the greatest men have suffered most.

14

Today, humanity is bowed down with trouble, sorrow and grief, no one escapes; the world is wet with tears; but, thank God, the remedy is at our doors. Let us turn our hearts away from the world of matter and live in the spiritual world! It alone can give us freedom! If we are hemmed in by difficulties we have only to call upon God, and by His great Mercy we shall be helped.

15

Whatsoever may happen is for the best, because affliction is but the essence of bounty, and sorrow and toil are mercy unalloyed, and anguish is peace of mind, and to make a sacrifice is to receive a gift, and whatsoever may come to pass hath issued from God's grace.

16

Chaos and confusion are daily increasing in the world. They will attain such intensity as to render the frame of mankind unable to bear them. Then will men be awakened and become aware that religion is the impregnable stronghold and the manifest light of the world, and its laws, exhortations and teachings the source of life on earth.

SHOGHI EFFENDI

17

. . . how often we seem to forget the clear and repeated warnings of our beloved Master, Who, in particular during the concluding years of His mission on earth, laid stress on the "severe mental tests" that would inevitably sweep over His loved ones of the West—tests that would purge, purify and prepare them for their noble mission in life.

18

However severe the challenge, however multiple the tasks, however short the time, however somber the world outlook, however limited the material resources of a hard-pressed adolescent community, the untapped sources of celestial strength from which it can draw are measureless, in their potencies, and will unhesitatingly pour forth their energizing influences if the necessary daily effort be made and the required sacrifices be willingly accepted.

19

The long ages of infancy and childhood, through which the human race had to pass, have receded into the background. Humanity is now experiencing the commotions invariably associated with the most turbulent stage of its evolution, the stage of adolescence, when the impetuosity of youth and its vehemence reach their climax, and must gradually be superseded by the calmness, the wisdom, and the maturity that characterize the stage of manhood. Then will the human race reach that stature of ripeness which will enable it to acquire all the powers and capacities upon which its ultimate development must depend.

20

Humanity, torn with dissension and burning with hate, is crying at this hour for a fuller measure of that love which is born of God, that love which in the last resort will prove the one solvent of its incalculable difficulties and problems. Is it not incumbent upon us, whose hearts are aglow with love for Him, to make still greater effort, to manifest that love in all its purity and power in our dealings with our fellow-men?

21

The world is, in truth, moving on towards its destiny. The interdependence of the peoples and nations of the earth, whatever the leaders of the divisive forces of the world may say or do, is already an accomplished fact. Its unity in the economic sphere is now understood and recognized. The welfare of the part means the welfare of the whole, and the distress of the part brings distress to the whole. The Revelation of Bahá'u'lláh has, in His own words, "*lent a fresh impulse and set a new direction*" to this vast process now operating in the world. The fires lit by this great ordeal are the consequences of men's failure to recognize it. They are, moreover, hastening its consummation. Adversity, prolonged, worldwide, afflictive, allied to chaos and universal destruction, must needs convulse the nations, stir the conscience of the world, disillusion the masses, precipitate a radical change in the very conception of society, and coalesce ultimately the disjointed, the bleeding limbs of mankind into one body, single, organically united, and indivisible.

22

. . . Suffering, although an inescapable reality, can nevertheless be utilised as a means for the attainment of happiness. This is the interpretation given to it by all the prophets and saints who, in the midst of severe tests and trials, felt happy and joyous and experienced what is best and holiest in life.

THE UNIVERSAL HOUSE
OF JUSTICE

23

It must be realized that the isolation and despair from which so many suffer are products of an environment ruled by an all-pervasive materialism. And in this the friends must understand the ramifications of Bahá'u'lláh's statement that "the present-day order" must "be rolled up, and a new one spread out in its stead."

24

. . . there is reassurance in the knowledge that, amidst the disintegration, a new kind of collective life is taking shape which gives practical expression to all that is heavenly in human beings.

25

As the process of the disintegration of a lamentably defective world order gathers momentum in all parts of the planet, engendering hopelessness, confusion, hostility, and insecurity, the hearts of the friends everywhere must be assured, their eyes clear-sighted, their feet firm, as they work patiently and sacrificially to raise a new order in its stead.

26

In such an afflicted time, when mankind is bewildered and the wisest of men are perplexed as to the remedy, the people of Bahá, who have confidence in His unfailing grace and divine guidance, are assured that each of these tormenting trials has a cause, a purpose, and a definite result, and all are essential instruments for the establishment of the immutable Will of God on earth. In other words, on the one hand humanity is struck by the scourge of His chastisement which will inevitably bring together the scattered and vanquished tribes of the earth; and on the other, the weak few whom He has nurtured under the protection of His loving guidance are, in this formative age and period of transition, continuing to build amidst these tumultuous waves an impregnable stronghold which will be the sole remaining refuge for those lost multitudes. Therefore, the dear friends of God who have such a broad and clear vision before them are not perturbed by such events, nor are they panic-stricken by such thundering sounds, nor will they face such convulsions with fear and trepidation, nor

will they be deterred, even for a moment, from
fulfilling their sacred responsibilities.

27

The sufferings sustained by the Báb so as to arouse humanity to the responsibilities of its coming age of maturity were themselves indications of the intensity of the struggle necessary for the world's people to pass through the age of humanity's collective adolescence. Paradoxical as it may seem, this is a source of hope. The turmoil and crises of our time underlie a momentous transition in human affairs. Simultaneous processes of disintegration and integration have clearly been accelerating throughout the planet since the Báb appeared in Persia. That our Earth has contracted into a neighbourhood, no one can seriously deny. The world is being made new. Death pangs are yielding to birth pangs. The pain shall pass when members of the human race act upon the common recognition of their essential oneness. There is a light at the end of this tunnel of change beckoning humanity to the goal destined for it according to the testimonies recorded in all the Holy Books.

28

In society at large, alas, the symptoms of an ever-deepening malaise of the soul multiply and worsen. How striking that, as the peoples of the world suffer for want of the true remedy and turn fitfully from one false hope to another, you are collectedly refining an instrument that connects hearts with the Word of God eternal. How striking that, amid the cacophony of fixed opinions and opposing interests that grows everywhere more fierce, you are focused on drawing people together to build communities that are havens of unity. Far from disheartening you, let the world's prejudices and hostilities be reminders of how urgently souls all around you need the healing balm that you alone can present to them.

29

Bahá'ís are encouraged to see in the revolutionary changes taking place in every sphere of life the interaction of two fundamental processes. One is destructive in nature, while the other is integrative; both serve to carry humanity, each in its own way, along the path leading towards its full maturity. The operation of the former is everywhere apparent—in the vicissitudes that have afflicted time-honored institutions, in the impotence of leaders at all levels to mend the fractures appearing in the structure of society, in the dismantling of social norms that have long held in check unseemly passions, and in the despondency and indifference exhibited not only by individuals but also by entire societies that have lost any vital sense of purpose. Though devastating in their effects, the forces of disintegration tend to sweep away barriers that block humanity's progress, opening space for the process of integration to draw diverse groups together and disclosing new opportunities for cooperation and collaboration. Bahá'ís, of course, strive to align themselves, individually and collectively, with forces associated with the process of integration, which, they are confident, will continue to gain in strength, no matter how bleak the immediate horizons. Human affairs will be utterly reorganized, and an era of universal peace inaugurated.

30

Today the world is assailed by an array of destructive forces. Materialism, rooted in the West, has now spread to every corner of the planet, breeding, in the name of a strong global economy and human welfare, a culture of consumerism. It skillfully and ingeniously promotes a habit of consumption that seeks to satisfy the basest and most selfish desires, while encouraging the expenditure of wealth so as to prolong and exacerbate social conflict. How vain and foolish a worldview! And meanwhile, a rising tide of fundamentalism, bringing with it an exceedingly narrow understanding of religion and spirituality, continues to gather strength, threatening to engulf humanity in rigid dogmatism. In its most extreme form, it conditions the resolution of the problems of the world upon the occurrence of events derived from illogical and superstitious notions. It professes to uphold virtue yet, in practice, perpetuates oppression and greed. Among the deplorable results of the operation of such forces are a deepening confusion on the part of young people everywhere, a sense of hopelessness in the ranks of those who would drive progress, and the emergence of a myriad social maladies.

The key to resolving these social ills rests in the hands of a youthful generation convinced of the nobility of human beings; eagerly seeking a deeper understanding of the true purpose of existence; able to distinguish between divine religion and mere superstition; clear in the view of science and religion as two independent yet complementary systems of knowledge that propel human progress; conscious of and drawn to the beauty and power of unity in diversity; secure in the knowledge that real glory is to be found in service to one's country and to the peoples of the world; and mindful that the acquisition of wealth is praiseworthy only insofar as it is attained through just means and expended for benevolent purposes, for the promotion of knowledge and toward the common good.

31

The world in which our efforts are taking place is likewise undergoing profound changes. On the one hand, the vast network of agencies and individuals that promote understanding and cooperation among diverse peoples affirms ever more powerfully the growing recognition that the "earth is but one country, and mankind its citizens." On the other hand, it is equally clear that the world is moving through a period of social paralysis, tyranny and anarchy, a period marked by the widespread neglect of both governmental and personal responsibility, the ultimate consequences of which no one on earth can foresee. The effect of both developments, as Shoghi Effendi also pointed out, will be to awaken in the hearts of those who share this planet with us a longing for unity and justice that can be met only by the Cause of God.

32

. . . an essential characteristic of this physical world is that we are constantly faced with trials, tribulations, hardships and sufferings and that by overcoming them we achieve our moral and spiritual development; that we must seek to accomplish in the future what we may have failed to do in the past; that this is the way God tests His servants and we should look upon every failure or shortcoming as an opportunity to try again and to acquire a fuller consciousness of the Divine Will and purpose.

Hope for
Spiritual Growth

BAHÁ'U'LLÁH

1

Sorrow not if, in these days and on this earthly plane, things contrary to your wishes have been ordained and manifested by God, for days of blissful joy, of heavenly delight, are assuredly in store for you. Worlds, holy and spiritually glorious, will be unveiled to your eyes.

2

Take thou the step of the spirit, so that, swift as the twinkling of an eye, thou mayest flash through the wilds of remoteness and bereavement, attain the Riḍván of everlasting reunion, and in one breath commune with the heavenly Spirits.

3

If the fire of self overcome you, remember your own faults and not the faults of My creatures, inasmuch as every one of you knoweth his own self better than he knoweth others.

4

Illumine and hallow your hearts; let them not be profaned by the thorns of hate or the thistles of malice. Ye dwell in one world, and have been created through the operation of one Will. Blessed is he who mingleth with all men in a spirit of utmost kindliness and love.

5

Set all thy hope in God, and cleave tenaciously to His unfailing mercy. Who else but Him can enrich the destitute, and deliver the fallen from his abasement?

6

Arise, O people, and, by the power of God's might, resolve to gain the victory over your own selves, that haply the whole earth may be freed and sanctified from its servitude to the gods of its idle fancies. . . .

‘ABDU’L-BAHÁ

7

Wherefore must the loved ones of God, laboriously, with the waters of their striving, tend and nourish and foster this tree of hope. In whatsoever land they dwell, let them with a whole heart befriend and be companions to those who are either close to them, or far removed. Let them, with qualities like unto those of heaven, promote the institutions and the religion of God. Let them never lose heart, never be despondent, never feel afflicted. The more antagonism they meet, the more let them show their own good faith; the more torments and calamities they have to face, the more generously let them pass round the bounteous cup. Such is the spirit which will become the life of the world, such is the spreading light at its heart . . .

8

. . . Strive that your actions day by day may be beautiful prayers. Turn towards God, and seek always to do that which is right and noble. Enrich the poor, raise the fallen, comfort the sorrowful, bring healing to the sick, reassure the fearful, rescue the oppressed, bring hope to the hopeless, shelter the destitute!

9

It is clear that life in this fast-fading world is as fleeting and inconstant as the morning wind, and this being so, how fortunate are the great who leave a good name behind them, and the memory of a lifetime spent in the pathway of the good pleasure of God.

10

Life is a load which must be carried on while we are on earth, but the cares of the lower things of life should not be allowed to monopolize all the thoughts and aspirations of a human being. The heart's ambitions should ascend to a more glorious goal, mental activity should rise to higher levels!

11

. . . the human spirit, unless it be assisted by the spirit of faith, cannot become acquainted with the divine mysteries and the heavenly realities. It is like a mirror which, although clear, bright, and polished, is still in need of light. Not until a sunbeam falls upon it can it discover the divine mysteries.

As for the mind, it is the power of the human spirit. The spirit is as the lamp, and the mind as the light that shines from it. The spirit is as the tree, and the mind as the fruit. The mind is the perfection of the spirit and a necessary attribute thereof, even as the rays of the sun are an essential requirement of the sun itself.

12

If a man's thought is constantly aspiring towards heavenly subjects then does he become saintly; if on the other hand his thought does not soar, but is directed downwards to center itself upon the things of this world, he grows more and more material until he arrives at a state little better than that of a mere animal.

Thoughts may be divided into two classes:

(1st) Thought that belongs to the world of thought alone.

(2nd) Thought that expresses itself in action.

Some men and women glory in their exalted thoughts, but if these thoughts never reach the plane of action they remain useless: the power of thought is dependent on its manifestation in deeds.

13

When man's soul is rarified and cleansed, spiritual links are established, and from these bonds sensations felt by the heart are produced. The human heart resembleth a mirror. When this is purified human hearts are attuned and reflect one another, and thus spiritual emotions are generated.

14

You must manifest complete love and affection toward all mankind. Do not exalt yourselves above others, but consider all as your equals, recognizing them as the servants of one God. Know that God is compassionate toward all; therefore, love all from the depths of your hearts, prefer all religionists before yourselves, be filled with love for every race, and be kind toward the people of all nationalities.

15

For every era hath a spirit; the spirit of this illumined era lieth in the teachings of Bahá'u'lláh. For these lay the foundation of the oneness of the world of humanity and promulgate universal brotherhood. They are founded upon the unity of science and religion and upon investigation of truth. They uphold the principle that religion must be the cause of amity, union and harmony among men. They establish the equality of both sexes and propound economic principles which are for the happiness of individuals. They diffuse universal education, that every soul may as much as possible have a share of knowledge. They abrogate and nullify religious, racial, political, patriotic and economic prejudices and the like. Those teachings . . . are the cause of the illumination and the life of the world of humanity. Whoever promulgateth them will verily be assisted by the Kingdom of God.

SHOGHI EFFENDI

16

Life is a constant struggle, not only against forces around us, but above all against our own ego. We can never afford to rest on our own oars, for if we do, we soon see ourselves carried down stream again.

17

We must not only be patient with others, infinitely patient!, but also with our own poor selves, remembering that even the Prophets of God sometimes got tired and cried out in despair!

18

The gross materialism that engulfs the entire nation at the present hour; the attachment to worldly things that enshrouds the souls of men; the fear and anxieties that distract their minds; the pleasure and dissipations that fill their time, the prejudices and animosities that darken their outlook, the apathy and lethargy that paralyze their spiritual faculties—these are among the formidable obstacles that stand in the path of every would-be warrior in the service of Bahá'u'lláh, obstacles which he must battle against and surmount in his crusade for the redemption of his own countrymen.

19

The more we search for ourselves, the less likely we are to find ourselves; and the more we search for God, and to serve our fellow-men, the more profoundly will we become acquainted with ourselves, and the more inwardly assured. This is one of the great spiritual laws of life.

20

. . . not everyone achieves easily and rapidly the victory over self. What every believer, new or old, should realize is that the Cause has the spiritual power to re-create us if we make the effort to let that power influence us, and the greatest help in this respect is prayer. We must supplicate Bahá'u'lláh to assist us to overcome the failings in our own characters, and also exert our own will power in mastering ourselves.

21

Ours then is the duty and privilege to labour, by day, by night, amidst the storm and stress of these troublous days, that we may quicken the zeal of our fellow-man, rekindle their hopes, stimulate their interests, open their eyes to the true Faith of God and enlist their active support in the carrying out of our common task for the peace and regeneration of the world.

22

. . . How to attain spirituality is indeed a question to which every young man and woman must sooner or later try to find a satisfactory answer. It is precisely because no such satisfactory answer has been given or found, that the modern youth finds itself bewildered, and is being consequently, carried away by the materialistic forces that are so powerfully undermining the foundations of man's moral and spiritual life. . . It is this condition so sadly morbid, into which society has fallen, that religion seeks to improve and transform.

For the core of religious faith is that mystic feeling which unites man with God. This state of spiritual communion can be brought about and maintained by means of meditation and prayer. And this is the reason why Bahá'u'lláh has so much stressed the importance of worship.

THE UNIVERSAL HOUSE
OF JUSTICE

23

Let no excessive self-criticism or any feelings of inadequacy, inability or inexperience hinder you or cause you to be afraid. Bury your fears in the assurances of Bahá'u'lláh. Has He not asserted that upon anyone who mentions His Name will descend the "hosts of Divine inspiration" and that on such a one will also descend the "Concourse on high, each bearing aloft a chalice of pure light"?

24

For outward developments to properly endure and flourish, they must be matched by inner spiritual growth. The process of drawing ever closer to Bahá'u'lláh in prayer and meditation, of deepening your grasp and appreciation of the fundamental verities of our Faith, of transforming your personal lives and conduct and fostering strong bonds of unity and love among the believers will enable you to reach unimagined heights and lay the foundation for a rich and active community life which, by its example, will draw the souls of others to its blissful shelter.

25

Alas, notwithstanding the laudable efforts, in every land, of well-intentioned individuals working to improve circumstances in society, the obstacles preventing the realization of such a vision seem insurmountable to many. Their hopes founder on erroneous assumptions about human nature that so permeate the structures and traditions of much of present-day living as to have attained the status of established fact. These assumptions appear to make no allowance for the extraordinary reservoir of spiritual potential available to any illumined soul who draws upon it; instead, they rely for justification on humanity's failings, examples of which daily reinforce a common sense of despair. A layered veil of false premises thus obscures a fundamental truth: The state of the world reflects a distortion of the human spirit, not its essential nature. The purpose of every Manifestation of God is to effect a transformation in both the inner life and external conditions of humanity. And this transformation naturally occurs as a growing body of people, united by the divine precepts, collectively seeks to develop spiritual capacities to contribute to a process of societal change.

26

The Holy Word has been extolled by the Prophets of God as the medium of celestial power and the wellspring of all spiritual, social and material progress. Access to it, constant study of it and daily use of it in our individual lives are vital to the inner personal transformation towards which we strive and whose ultimate outer manifestation will be the emergence of that divine civilization which is the promise of the World Order of Bahá'u'lláh.

27

The well-being of humanity is a reflection of its spiritual state, and any enduring change for the better in its material affairs requires a change in its spiritual condition. For this reason the principal concern and contribution of the followers of Bahá'u'lláh is the spiritual transformation of human society, with full confidence that by this means they are making a most valuable and most fundamental contribution to the betterment of the world and the rectification of its many problems.

28

Let each believer in his inmost heart resolve not to be seduced by the ephemeral allurements of the society around him, nor to be drawn into its feuds and short-lived enthusiasms, but instead to transfer all he can from the old world to that new one which is the vision of his longing and will be the fruit of his labors.

Hope for the Future—
Peace, Unity, & Justice

BAHÁ'U'LLÁH

1

This is the Day in which God's most excellent favors have been poured out upon men, the Day in which His most mighty grace hath been infused into all created things. It is incumbent upon all the peoples of the world to reconcile their differences, and, with perfect unity and peace, abide beneath the shadow of the Tree of His care and loving-kindness. It behooveth them to cleave to whatsoever will, in this Day, be conducive to the exaltation of their stations, and to the promotion of their best interests.

2

The purpose of religion as revealed from the heaven of God's holy Will is to establish unity and concord amongst the peoples of the world; make it not the cause of dissension and strife. The religion of God and His divine law are the most potent instruments and the surest of all means for the dawning of the light of unity amongst men. The progress of the world, the development of nations, the tranquility of peoples, and the peace of all who dwell on earth are among the principles and ordinances of God.

3

This is the Day whereon the Ocean of God's mercy hath been manifested unto men, the Day in which the Daystar of His loving-kindness hath shed its radiance upon them, the Day in which the clouds of His bountiful favor have overshadowed the whole of mankind. Now is the time to cheer and refresh the down-cast through the invigorating breeze of love and fellowship, and the living waters of friendliness and charity.

4

No light can compare with the light of justice. The establishment of order in the world and the tranquillity of the nations depend upon it.

5

O contending peoples and kindreds of the earth! Set your faces towards unity, and let the radiance of its light shine upon you. Gather ye together, and for the sake of God resolve to root out whatever is the source of contention amongst you.

6

The first utterance of Him Who is the All-Wise is this: O children of dust! Turn your faces from the darkness of estrangement to the effulgent light of the daystar of unity. This is that which above all else will benefit the peoples of the earth. O friend! Upon the tree of utterance there hath never been, nor shall there ever be, a fairer leaf, and beneath the ocean of knowledge no pearl more wondrous can ever be found.

7

Justice is, in this day, bewailing its plight, and Equity groaneth beneath the yoke of oppression. The thick clouds of tyranny have darkened the face of the earth, and enveloped its peoples. Through the movement of Our Pen of glory We have, at the bidding of the omnipotent Ordainer, breathed a new life into every human frame, and instilled into every word a fresh potency. All created things proclaim the evidences of this worldwide regeneration. This is the most great, the most joyful tidings imparted by the Pen of this wronged One to mankind.

8

The whole earth is now in a state of pregnancy. The day is approaching when it will have yielded its noblest fruits, when from it will have sprung forth the loftiest trees, the most enchanting blossoms, the most heavenly blessings.

‘ABDU’L-BAHÁ

9

Rest thou assured that in this era of the spirit, the Kingdom of Peace will raise up its tabernacle on the summits of the world, and the commandments of the Prince of Peace will so dominate the arteries and nerves of every people as to draw into His sheltering shade all the nations on earth. From springs of love and truth and unity will the true Shepherd give His sheep to drink.

O handmaid of God, peace must first be established among individuals, until it leadeth in the end to peace among nations. Wherefore, O ye Bahá'ís, strive ye with all your might to create, through the power of the Word of God, genuine love, spiritual communion and durable bonds among individuals. This is your task.

10

Do not allow your minds to dwell on the present, but with eyes of faith look into the future, for in truth the Spirit of God is working in your midst.

11

Look ye not upon the present, fix your gaze upon the times to come. In the beginning, how small is the seed, yet in the end it is a mighty tree. Look ye not upon the seed, look ye upon the tree, and its blossoms, and its leaves and its fruits.

12

Lift up your hearts above the present and look with eyes of faith into the future! Today the seed is sown, the grain falls upon the earth, but behold the day will come when it shall rise a glorious tree and the branches thereof shall be laden with fruit. Rejoice and be glad that this day has dawned, try to realize its power, for it is indeed wonderful! God has crowned you with honor and in your hearts has He set a radiant star; verily the light thereof shall brighten the whole world!

13

. . . as to religious, racial, national and political bias: all these prejudices strike at the very root of human life; one and all they beget bloodshed, and the ruination of the world. So long as these prejudices survive, there will be continuous and fearsome wars.

To remedy this condition there must be universal peace. To bring this about, a Supreme Tribunal must be established, representative of all governments and peoples; questions both national and international must be referred thereto, and all must carry out the decrees of this Tribunal. Should any government or people disobey, let the whole world arise against that government or people.

14

As the teachings of Bahá'u'lláh are combined with universal peace, they are like a table provided with every kind of fresh and delicious food. Every soul can find, at that table of infinite bounty, that which he desires. If the question is restricted to universal peace alone, the remarkable results which are expected and desired will not be attained. The scope of universal peace must be such that all the communities and religions may find their highest wish realized in it. The teachings of Bahá'u'lláh are such that all the communities of the world, whether religious, political or ethical, ancient or modern, find in them the expression of their highest wish.

15

. . . every great Cause in this world of existence findeth visible expression through three means: first, intention; second, confirmation; third, action. Today on this earth there are many souls who are promoters of peace and reconciliation and are longing for the realization of the oneness and unity of the world of humanity; but this intention needeth a dynamic power, so that it may become manifest in the world of being. In this day the divine instructions and lordly exhortations promulgate this most great aim, and the confirmations of the Kingdom also support and aid the realization of this intention. Therefore, although the combined forces and thoughts of the nations of the world cannot by themselves achieve this exalted purpose, the power of the Word of God penetrateth all things and the assistance of the divine Kingdom is continuous. Erelong it will become evident and clear that the ensign of the Most Great Peace is the teachings of Bahá'u'lláh, and the tent of union and harmony among nations is the Tabernacle of the divine Kingdom, for therein the intention, the power and the action, all three, are brought together. The realization of everything in the world of being dependeth upon these three elements.

16

The bulk of humanity now realiseth what a great calamity war is and how war turneth man into a ferocious animal, causing prosperous cities and villages to be reduced to ruins and the foundations of the human edifice to crumble. Now, since all men have been awakened and their ears are attentive, it is time for the promulgation of universal peace—a peace based on righteousness and justice—that mankind may not be exposed to further dangers in the future. Now is the dawn of universal peace, and the first streaks of its light are beginning to appear. We earnestly hope that its effulgent orb may shine forth and flood the East and the West with its radiance. The establishment of universal peace is not possible save through the power of the Word of God. . . .

17

War and its ravages have blighted the world; the education of woman will be a mighty step toward its abolition and ending, for she will use her whole influence against war.

18

All of us know that international peace is good, that it is conducive to human welfare and the glory of man, but volition and action are necessary before it can be established.

19

My hope is that through the zeal and ardour of the pure of heart, the darkness of hatred and difference will be entirely abolished, and the light of love and unity shall shine; this world shall become a new world; things material shall become the mirror of the divine; human hearts shall meet and embrace each other; the whole world become as a man's native country and the different races be counted as one race.

20

The constellation of love and wisdom and power is once more shining from the Divine Horizon to give joy to all who turn their faces to the Light of God. Bahá'u'lláh has rent the veil of prejudice and superstition which was stirring the souls of men. Let us pray to God that the breath of the Holy Spirit may again give hope and refreshment to the people, awakening in them a desire to do the Will of God. May heart and soul be vivified in every man: so will they all rejoice in a new birth.

21

Today the one overriding need is unity and harmony among the beloved of the Lord, for they should have among them but one heart and soul and should, so far as in them lieth, unitedly withstand the hostility of all the peoples of the world; they must bring to an end the benighted prejudices of all nations and religions and must make known to every member of the human race that all are the leaves of one branch, the fruits of one bough.

22

I shall ask you a question: Did God create us for love or for enmity? Did He create us for peace or discord? Surely He has created us for love; therefore, we should live in accordance with His will. Do not listen to anything that is prejudiced, for self-interest prompts men to be prejudiced.

23

Today the world of humanity is in need of international unity and conciliation. To establish these great fundamental principles a propelling power is needed. It is self-evident that the unity of the human world and the Most Great Peace cannot be accomplished through material means. They cannot be established through political power, for the political interests of nations are various and the policies of peoples are divergent and conflicting. They cannot be founded through racial or patriotic power, for these are human powers, selfish and weak. The very nature of racial differences and patriotic prejudices prevents the realization of this unity and agreement. Therefore, it is evidenced that the promotion of the oneness of the kingdom of humanity, which is the essence of the teachings of all the Manifestations of God, is impossible except through the divine power and breaths of the Holy Spirit. Other powers are too weak and are incapable of accomplishing this.

24

The earth has one surface. God has not divided this surface by boundaries and barriers to separate races and peoples. Man has set up and established these imaginary lines, giving to each restricted area a name and the limitation of a native land or nationhood. By this division and separation into groups and branches of mankind, prejudice is engendered which becomes a fruitful source of war and strife. Impelled by this prejudice, races and nations declare war against each other; the blood of the innocent is poured out, and the earth torn by violence. Therefore, it has been decreed by God in this day that these prejudices and differences shall be laid aside. All are commanded to seek the good pleasure of the Lord of unity, to follow His command and obey His will; in this way the world of humanity shall become illumined with the reality of love and reconciliation.

25

Daughters and sons must follow the same curriculum of study, thereby promoting unity of the sexes. When all mankind shall receive the same opportunity of education and the equality of men and women be realized, the foundations of war will be utterly destroyed. Without equality this will be impossible because all differences and distinction are conducive to discord and strife.

26

The world of humanity is possessed of two wings: the male and the female. So long as these two wings are not equivalent in strength, the bird will not fly. Until womankind reaches the same degree as man, until she enjoys the same arena of activity, extraordinary attainment for humanity will not be realized; humanity cannot wing its way to heights of real attainment. When the two wings or parts become equivalent in strength, enjoying the same prerogatives, the flight of man will be exceedingly lofty and extraordinary. Therefore, woman must receive the same education as man and all inequality be adjusted. Thus, imbued with the same virtues as man, rising through all the degrees of human attainment, women will become the peers of men, and until this equality is established, true progress and attainment for the human race will not be facilitated.

27

Justice is not limited, it is a universal quality. Its operation must be carried out in all classes, from the highest to the lowest. Justice must be sacred, and the rights of all the people must be considered. Desire for others only that which you desire for yourselves. Then shall we rejoice in the Sun of Justice, which shines from the Horizon of God.

SHOGHI EFFENDI

28

God's purpose is none other than to usher in, in ways He alone can bring about, and the full significance of which He alone can fathom, the Great, the Golden Age of a long-divided, a long-afflicted humanity. Its present state, indeed even its immediate future, is dark, distressingly dark. Its distant future, however, is radiant, gloriously radiant—so radiant that no eye can visualize it.

29

The enormous energy dissipated and wasted on war, whether economic or political, will be consecrated to such ends as will extend the range of human inventions and technical development, to the increase of the productivity of mankind, to the extermination of disease, to the extension of scientific research, to the raising of the standard of physical health, to the sharpening and refinement of the human brain, to the exploitation of the unused and unsuspected resources of the planet, to the prolongation of human life, and to the furtherance of any other agency that can stimulate the intellectual, the moral, and spiritual life of the entire human race.

30

The proclamation of the Oneness of Mankind—the head cornerstone of Bahá'u'-lláh's all-embracing dominion—can under no circumstances be compared with such expressions of pious hope as have been uttered in the past. His is not merely a call which He raised, alone and unaided, in the face of the relentless and combined opposition of two of the most powerful Oriental potentates of His day—while Himself an exile and prisoner in their hands. It implies at once a warning and a promise—a warning that in it lies the sole means for the salvation of a greatly suffering world, a promise that its realization is at hand.

31

No doubt in the future, when the foundation of society is laid according to the Divine plan, and men become truly spiritualized, a vast amount of our present ills and problems will be remedied. We who toil now are paving the way for a far better world, and this knowledge must uphold and strengthen us through every trial.

32

It is becoming evident that the world is not yet through with its labour, the New Age not yet fully born, real Peace not yet right round the corner. We must have no illusions about how much depends on us and our success or failure. All humanity is disturbed and suffering and confused; we cannot expect to not be disturbed and not to suffer—but we don't have to be confused. On the contrary, confidence and assurance, hope and optimism are our prerogative. The successful carrying out of our various Plans is the greatest sign we can give of our faith and inner assurance, and the best way we can help our fellow-men out of their confusion and difficulties.

THE UNIVERSAL HOUSE
OF JUSTICE

33

As humanity passes through the age of transition in its evolution to a world civilization which will be illuminated by spiritual values and will be distinguished by its justice and its unity, the role of the Bahá'í community is clear: it must accomplish a spiritual transformation of its members, and must offer to the world a model of the society destined to come into being through the power of the Revelation of Bahá'u'lláh.

34

In the Revelation of Bahá'u'lláh, the nobility inherent to every human being is unequivocally asserted; it is a fundamental tenet of Bahá'í belief, upon which hope for the future of humankind is built. The soul's capacity to manifest all the names and attributes of God—He Who is the Compassionate, the Bestower, the Bountiful—is repeatedly affirmed in the Writings. Economic life is an arena for the expression of honesty, integrity, trustworthiness, generosity, and other qualities of the spirit. The individual is not merely a self-interested economic unit, striving to claim an ever-greater share of the world's material resources. "Man's merit lieth in service and virtue," Bahá'u'lláh avers, "and not in the pageantry of wealth and riches." And further: "Dissipate not the wealth of your precious lives in the pursuit of evil and corrupt affection, nor let your endeavours be spent in promoting your personal interest." By consecrating oneself to the service of others, one finds meaning and purpose in life and contributes to the upliftment of society itself.

35

The light of the Revelation is destined to illumine every sphere of endeavour; in each, the relationships that sustain society are to be recast; in each, the world seeks examples of how human beings should be to one another. We offer for your consideration, given its conspicuous part in generating the ferment in which so many people have recently been embroiled, the economic life of humanity, where injustice is tolerated with indifference and disproportionate gain is regarded as the emblem of success. So deeply entrenched are such pernicious attitudes that it is hard to imagine how any one individual can alone alter the prevailing standards by which the relationships in this domain are governed. Nevertheless, there are certainly practices a Bahá'í would eschew, such as dishonesty in one's transactions or the economic exploitation of others. Faithful adherence to the divine admonitions demands there be no contradiction between one's economic conduct and one's beliefs as a Bahá'í. By applying in one's life those principles of the Faith that relate to fairness and equity, a single soul can uphold a standard far above the low threshold by which the world measures itself. Humanity is weary for want of a pattern of life to which to aspire; we look to you to foster communities whose ways will give hope to the world.

36

. . . you are well aware of your mission to be a source of hope to those around you, to be channels of love and affection, to be symbols of forgiveness and patience, of serenity and strength to your compatriots, and above all, to be in the front ranks of that process by which the worldwide community has learned to build capacity for service, heighten unity, deepen understanding, and hone abilities so that purposeful action for the benefit of mankind may ensue.

NOTES

Hope Through Hardship & Global Unrest

BAHÁ'U'LLÁH

1. The Hidden Words, Arabic no. 50.
2. Epistle to the Son of the Wolf, p. 17.
3. *The Proclamation of Bahá'u'lláh,* p. 118.
4. *Tablets of Bahá'u'lláh revealed after the Kitáb-i-Aqdas,* p. 69.

'ABDU'L-BAHÁ

5. *Selections from the Writings of 'Abdu'l-Bahá,* no. 178.1.
6. Ibid., no. 35.12.
7. *The Promulgation of Universal Peace,* p. 74.
8. *Eternal Beloved,* p. 12.
9. *Selections from the Writings of 'Abdu'l-Bahá,* no. 150.3.
10. *Eternal Beloved,* pp. 13–14.

11. 'Abdu'l-Bahá, "Extract from a Tablet of 'Abdu'l-Bahá," https://www.bahai.org/library/authoritative-texts/abdul-baha/additional-tablets-extracts-talks/852331321/852331321.xhtml?fbe077e9.

12. *Selections from the Writings of 'Abdu'l-Bahá*, no. 22.1.

13. *Paris Talks*, no. 57.1.

14. Ibid., no. 35.7.

15. *Selections from the Writings of 'Abdu'l-Bahá*, no. 200.10.

16. From a Tablet—translated from the Persian, in "Peace," no. 26, https://bahai-library.org/writings/bahaullah/aqdas/aqdas2/Compilations/Peace/26.htm.

SHOGHI EFFENDI

17. *Bahá'í Administration*, p. 50.

18. *Citadel of Faith*, p. 85.

19. *The World Order of Bahá'u'lláh*, p. 202.

20. *Bahá'í Administration*, p. 62.

21. *The Promised Day Is Come*, ¶300.

22. From a letter written on behalf of Shoghi Effendi to an individual believer, May 29, 1932, in *Lights of Guidance*, no. 944.

THE UNIVERSAL HOUSE OF JUSTICE

23. *Messages from the Universal House of Justice, 2001–2022*, no. 164.33.

24. Ibid., no. 240.3.

25. Ibid., no. 315.1.

26. *Messages from the Universal House of Justice, 1963–1986,* no. 246.5.

27. *Messages from the Universal House of Justice, 2001–2022,* no. 2.4.

28. Ibid., no. 259.5.

29. Ibid., no. 195.4.

30. Ibid., no. 152.9–10.

31. Ibid., no. 3.8.

32. From a letter written on behalf of the Universal House of Justice to an individual believer, January 9, 1977, in *Lights of Guidance,* no. 1226.

Hope for Spiritual Growth

BAHÁ'U'LLÁH

1. *Gleanings from the Writings of Bahá'u'lláh,* no. 153.9.

2. The Kitáb-i-Íqán: The Book of Certitude, ¶44.

3. The Hidden Words, Persian no. 66.

4. *Gleanings from the Writings of Bahá'u'lláh,* no. 156.1.

5. Ibid., 153.1.

6. Ibid., 43.3.

'ABDU'L-BAHÁ

7. *Selections from the Writings of 'Abdu'l-Bahá,* no. 206.13.

8. *Paris Talks,* no. 26.7.

9. *The Secret of Divine Civilization,* ¶127.

10. *Paris Talks,* no. 31.9.

11. *Some Answered Questions,* no. 55.5–55.6.

12. *Paris Talks,* no. 2.2–2.6.

13. *Selections from the Writings of 'Abdu'l-Bahá,* no. 70.5.

14. *The Promulgation of Universal Peace,* p. 638.

15. *Selections from the Writings of 'Abdu'l-Bahá,* no. 71.1.

SHOGHI EFFENDI

16. *Unfolding Destiny,* p. 454.

17. Ibid., p. 456.

18. *Citadel of Faith,* p. 149.

19. From a letter written on behalf of Shoghi Effendi to an individual believer, February 18, 1954, in *Lights of Guidance,* no. 391.

20. From a letter written on behalf of Shoghi Effendi to an individual believer, January 27, 1945, in *Lights of Guidance,* no. 394.

21. From a letter written by Shoghi Effendi to the believers in Australia and New Zealand, December 2, 1923, in *Lights of Guidance,* no. 450.

22. From a letter of the Guardian to an individual believer, December 8, 1935, in *Lights of Guidance,* no. 1845.

THE UNIVERSAL HOUSE OF JUSTICE

23. *Messages from the Universal House of Justice, 1986–2001*, no. 200.12.

24. Ibid., no. 301.3

25. *Messages from the Universal House of Justice, 2001–2022*, no. 187.3.

26. *Messages from the Universal House of Justice, 1986–2001*, no. 68.1.

27. Ibid., no. 96.4.

28. *Messages from the Universal House of Justice, 1963–1986*, no. 13.7.

Hope for the Future— Peace, Unity & Justice

BAHÁ'U'LLÁH

1. *Gleanings from the Writings of Bahá'u'lláh*, no. 4.1.

2. *Tablets of Bahá'u'lláh revealed after the Kitáb-i-Aqdas*, no. 8.60.

3. *Gleanings from the Writings of Bahá'u'lláh*, no. 5.1.

4. Epistle to the Son of the Wolf, pp. 28–29.

5. *Gleanings from the Writings of Bahá'u'lláh*, no. 111.1.

6. *The Pen of Glory*, no. 2.10.

7. *Gleanings from the Writings of Bahá'u'lláh*, no. 43.2.

8. Quoted in Shoghi Effendi, *The Promised Day Is Come*, p. 75.

ABDU'L-BAHÁ

9. *Selections from the Writings of 'Abdu'l-Bahá*, no. 201.1–2.
10. *Paris Talks*, no. 53.5.
11. *Selections from the Writings of 'Abdu'l-Bahá*, no. 40.3.
12. *Paris Talks*, no. 21.6.
13. *Selections from the Writings of 'Abdu'l-Bahá*, no. 202.10–11.
14. Ibid., no. 227.25.
15. From a Tablet—translated from Persian, in "Peace," no. 24, https://bahai-library.org/writings/bahaullah/aqdas/aqdas2/Compilations/Peace/24.htm.
16. Ibid., no. 25.
17. *The Promulgation of Universal Peace*, p. 149.
18. Ibid., p. 167.
19. *'Abdu'l-Bahá in London*, p. 38.
20. *Paris Talks*, no. 8.7.
21. *Selections from the Writings of 'Abdu'l-Bahá*, no. 221.4.
22. *The Promulgation of Universal Peace*, p. 57.
23. Ibid., pp. 15–16.
24. Ibid., pp. 449–50.
25. Ibid., p. 243.
26. Ibid., p. 529.
27. *Paris Talks*, no. 49.15.

SHOGHI EFFENDI

28. *The Promised Day Is Come,* ¶286.
29. *The World Order of Bahá'u'lláh,* p. 204.
30. Ibid., p. 47.
31. From a letter written on behalf of Shoghi Effendi to an individual believer, March 3, 1943, in *Lights of Guidance,* no. 2049.
32. From a letter dated 9 April 1949 written on behalf of Shoghi Effendi to an individual believer, in *Unfolding Destiny,* p. 225.

THE UNIVERSAL HOUSE OF JUSTICE

33. *Messages from the Universal House of Justice, 1986–2001,* no. 149.18.
34. *Messages from the Universal House of Justice, 2001–2022,* no. 278.6.
35. Ibid., no. 187.7.
36. Ibid., no. 220.5.

BIBLIOGRAPHY

Works of Bahá'u'lláh

Epistle to the Son of the Wolf. New ed. Translated by
Shoghi Effendi. 1st ps ed. Wilmette, IL:
Bahá'í Publishing Trust, 1988.

Gleanings from the Writings of Bahá'u'lláh. Translated by Shoghi Effendi. Wilmette, IL:
Bahá'í Publishing, 2005.

The Hidden Words. Translated by Shoghi Effendi.
Wilmette, IL: Bahá'í Publishing, 2002.

The Kitáb-i-Íqán: The Book of Certitude. Translated
by Shoghi Effendi. Wilmette, IL: Bahá'í
Publishing, 2003.

The Pen of Glory: Selected Works of Bahá'u'lláh. Wilmette, IL: Bahá'í Publishing, 2008.

The Proclamation of Bahá'u'lláh. Wilmette, IL:
Bahá'í Publishing Trust, 1978.

Tablets of Bahá'u'lláh revealed after the Kitáb-i-Aqdas. Compiled by the Research Department of the Universal House of Justice. Translated by Habib Taherzadeh et al. Wilmette, IL: Bahá'í Publishing Trust, 1988.

Works of 'Abdu'l-Bahá

'Abdu'l-Bahá in London: Addresses and Notes of Conversations. London: Bahá'í Publishing Trust, 1982.

Eternal Beloved: Prayers of 'Abdu'l-Bahá. Wilmette, IL: Bahá'í Publishing, 2021.

"Extract from a Tablet of 'Abdu'l-Bahá," https://www.bahai.org/library/authoritative-texts/abdul-baha/additional-tablets-extracts-tal ks/852331321/852331321.xhtml?f-be077e9.

Paris Talks: Addresses Given By 'Abdu'l-Bahá in Paris in 1911. Wilmette, IL: Bahá'í Publishing, 2011.

Promulgation of Universal Peace: Talks Delivered by 'Abdu'l-Bahá during His Visit to the United States and Canada in 1912. Compiled by Howard MacNutt. Wilmette, IL: Bahá'í Publishing, 2012.

The Secret of Divine Civilization. Translated by Marzieh Gail and Ali-Kuli Khan. Wilmette, IL: Bahá'í Publishing, 2007.

Selections from the Writings of 'Abdu'l-Bahá. Compiled by the Research Department of the Universal House of Justice. Translated by a Committee at the Bahá'í World Center and Marzieh Gail. Wilmette, IL: Bahá'í Publishing, 2010.

Some Answered Questions. Compiled and translated from the Persian by Laura Clifford Barney. Newly Revised by a Committee at the Bahá'í World Center. Reprinted with the permission of the Bahá'í World Center. Wilmette, IL: Bahá'í Publishing, 2014.

Works of Shoghi Effendi

Bahá'í Administration. Wilmette, IL: Bahá'í Publishing Trust, 1998.

Citadel of Faith. Wilmette, IL: Bahá'í Publishing Trust, 2014.

The Promised Day Is Come. 1st pocket-size ed. Wilmette, IL: Bahá'í Publishing Trust, 1996.

Unfolding Destiny: The Messages from the Guardian of the Bahá'í Faith to the Bahá'í Community of the British Isles. London: Bahá'í Publishing Trust, 1981.

The World Order of Bahá'u'lláh: Selected Letters. New ed. Wilmette, IL: Bahá'í Publishing Trust, 1991.

Works of the Universal House of Justice

Messages from the Universal House of Justice, 1963–1986: The Third Epoch of the Formative Age. Compiled by Geoffry Marks. Wilmette, IL: Bahá'í Publishing Trust, 1996.

Messages from the Universal House of Justice, 1986–2001: The Fourth Epoch of the Formative Age. Wilmette, IL: Bahá'í Publishing Trust, 2010.

Messages from the Universal House of Justice, 2001–2022: The Fifth Epoch of the Formative Age. Evanston, IL: Bahá'í Publishing, 2024.

Bahá'í Compilations

Lights of Guidance: A Bahá'í Reference File. Compiled by Helen Hornby. New ed. New Delhi, India: Bahá'í Publishing Trust, 1994.

"Peace." Compiled by the Research Department of the Universal House of Justice. August, 1985. Revised September, 1990. https://bahai-library.org/writings/bahaullah/aqdas/aqdas2/Compilations/Peace/StartPage.htm.